GRINNIN', DUSTY, FIGHTIN' MEN

"... fightin' men who bear the name Marine."

GRINNIN', DUSTY, FIGHTIN' MEN

and other ballads about the Marines

by

Colonel Grant Dunnagan
United States Marine Corps (Retired)

Shelley Books
Raleigh, North Carolina
1985

Published in 1985 by Shelley Books
Box 17184, North Hills Station
Raleigh, North Carolina 27619

ISBN 0-961-51880-4

Printed in the United States of America.

CONTENTS

Dedicated with pride and admiration to the United States Marines; and especially to those of Air Warning Squadron 8, Second Marine Air Wing -- WW II; and of the 3rd Platoon, "Bloody George" Company, 3rd Bn., First Marines -- Korean Conflict; and of the III Marine Amphibious Force--Vietnam; and to the fourth Marine my clan has given the Corps, Captain Michael Grant Dunnagan.

GRINNIN', DUSTY, FIGHTIN' MEN

We'd just come back to garrison
                     from China's dusty plain,
When the clackin' of a metal key
                     sent us out again.

This time it was a bandit raid that
                     turned us out of bed.
They'd massacred a mission post
                     the wireless message said.

Drums beat a staccato roll that
                     marked the end of night,
And bugles tattooed sweet and clear
                     in China's early light.

"Right by twos and dress it up,"
                     barked old Sergeant Hart,
And out we cantered through the gate
                     high spirited and smart.

1

Peking Legation's pride and joy,
                            we did a first-rate job,
Despite the taunts of foot Marines
                     who called us "Mongol Mob."

We uniformed the same as they, in
                         khakis, blues, and greens;
But we were Peking's Finest--
                     the vaunted Horse Marines.

The foot Marines stood sleepily
                   beneath their heavy packs,
Faces dark and sullen as they
                   watched our jouncing backs.

You couldn't rightly blame them, for
                       frequently they'd find
We'd had the heart out of a fight, and
                     left them just the rind.

But that was just the way of it, for
                             marchin's never fast;
So we were always first on hand; the
                             foot troops always last.

And now the dusty road flew under
                             hooves like drumming rain;
And long before the foot troops came, our
                             dust was down again.

The scarlet guidon dipped and danced
                             up at the column's head,
Its golden facings cheery-bright
                             against the field of red.

The silver guidon tip picked up the
                             rising sun's first light
And threw it back in steady pulses,
                             flashing lightning-bright.

Mongol bandits still were there when
                we had finished our ride,
And we swung into a skirmish line
                without breaking stride.

The noonday sun was overhead when
                we began the fight,
Each man among us sure he'd see
                Peking again 'fore night.

For bandits were only rabble, who
                knew scant discipline;
One charge through and back again would
                leave their ranks damn' thin.

So in we went at a gallop, firing
                over our horses' heads,
Thinkin' this might be fun enough for
                leavin' our warm beds.

For we all thought that bandit gang
                    would stand and make a fight;
Instead they disappeared like bats
                    will vanish in the night.

They raced out from the mission in a
                    ragged, scattered line,
With us a rifle-shot behind, our
                    spirits high and fine.

A'sudden, where the hills began, they
                    wheeled into the brush;
And we were forced to rein up hard,
                    for fear of an ambush.

Our scouts moved forward at slow-walk,
                    and then they went afoot.
And at about three hundred yards
                    those Chinks began to shoot.

And now we all had to dismount and
                        fight from tree to tree,
For wooded, hilly real estate's
                        no place for cavalry.

Astride our horses, sittin' tall,
                        we counted each man two;
But sluggin' in as infantry, we
                        numbered far too few.

Bandits were all about us; you could
                        almost hear "Taps" trill.
We were runnin' out of ammo and
                        surrounded on that hill.

When 'round the bend and up the road,
                        a pretty sight to see,
Came those grinnin', dusty, fightin' men --
                        Marine Corps infantry!

"Infantry's Queen of Battle," I'd
                    heard it said before;
And since that lonely Chinese hill
                    I'll preach it evermore.

Of course, we couldn't tell *them* that,
                    we said 'twas just a job;
And we bristled just as fiercely when
                    they called us "Mongol Mob".

But it was always comforting
                    to know they'd be along,
These men who walk to battle with
                    a cuss word and a song.

For no finer host has soldiered
                    since warring first began,
Than those described by Thomason's,
                  "Drilled shoulders...bone-deep tan."

Any place they serve, they're
true sons of "Battle's Queen",
Those grinnin', dusty, fightin' men
who bear the name "Marine".

THE BAPTISM OF JOHNNY CREW

Johnny Crew, the replacement, came
   with a thousand questions, or two;
And he asked them all of the Gunny
   just the same as me or you.

"Oh, why are the drums so quiet now
   and why don't the bandsmen play?"
"They're tired, bone tired, from fightin';
   they've made grisly music this day."

"Why are we movin' out again
   when it's drawin' so close to night?"
"Because the fight won't come to us,
   so we must go to the fight."

"What's that sound like hammerin'
                across the valleys ahead?"
"That's M-1's drivin' coffin nails,"
                the Gunnery Sergeant said.

"What's that along the skyline
                of the hill that juts so high?"
"That's enemy troops, waitin' for us;
                dead men, preparin' to die."

"And what is that sound about us now
                like a covey takin' flight?"
"It's 'whispering death' from the mortars;
                lie down and hug the earth tight."

"Why do our troopers lie so still, and
                    why do they look so white?"
"They've fought their last, poor devils;
                    they'll get their sleep tonight."

"Why do we move so slowly now
        and what are those splashes of red?"
"It's our hill now and the red, red snow
        is the bill marked 'paid' by our dead.

"We'll set up our defenses here
                    and get set for a pre-dawn fight,
for our real estate's been reassessed
        and the price will go up in the night."

11

"So keep your rifle from freezin'
and get some sleep if you can.
By this time tomorrow afternoon
you'll know you're a fightin' man."

THE PLACE FOR ME'S ARTILLERY

There's Air and Tanks and Infantry,
But the place for me's Artillery.

The big guns' blinding, sizzling, crash,
      the sudden glimpse of hell;
And swirling through the rolling boom,
      that brimstone-cordite smell.

Clouds of dust on half-made roads
      as batteries wheel into line,
And sweaty, dusty, cannoneers
      and barrels all a'shine.

Artillery, Artillery,
The place for me's Artillery.

Hurry! Move! No time to linger,
                get those bubbles level.
And get the trail legs sand-bagged in;
                race to beat the devil!

What's holdin' up there, Number Three?
                We haven't got all day!
Make it snappy! Ready? Up?
                Then, get those rounds away!

Artillery, Artillery,
The place for me's Artillery.

The powderbags pilin' high
                    in eerie battle-light,
While F O's scream for fire up front
                    throughout the hell-black night.

"End of mission; secure the guns",
                    but ask no sleep this night.
Dawn-pink's hangin' in the sky
                    and there's rounds to fire 'fore light.

      Artillery, Artillery,
      The place for me's Artillery.

The noonday sun will shine on us
                    stirrin' dust again,
For it's sudden death to stay too long
                    where cannon flash has been.

So, hurry! Move! No time to waste.
                Lay those big guns well,
And check your aimin' stakes again
                for a T.O.T. in hell!

There's Air and Tanks and Infantry,
But the place for me's Artillery!

IN THE LAND OF SAYONARA

At the foot of Fuji Mountain
               near the bright red Torii gates,
There's a Nippon girl who sits there
                  and patiently she waits.

Her up-tipped eyes are star shine,
               her hair is a midnight sky,
And her smile's the warmth of morning suns
               for a thousand years gone by.

We met in Fuji-san's shadow
                    where the silent waters wait,
In the land of Sayonara
                    by a lonely Torii gate.

And we loved for just a moment
                    that far too soon was lost,
When I sailed away and left her
                    for a different, distant post.

Now, lonely in the summer night
                    when gentle breezes sigh,
I sometimes hear her laughter
                    tinkling soft, nearby.

On guard post in the moonlight

                how often do I hear

Her plunking on the *samisen*,

            Strange music, sad and dear.

I watch the empty drill field;

            and she comes walking there,

Kimono bright as moonbeams

              that bend to touch her hair.

But I'm only seeing shadows

              however real they seem,

And a wind song is the music

              that haunts my lonely dream.

For we kissed 'neath Fuji Yama
and I left her standing there,
Tears in her dark eyes shining,
moonlight aglow in her hair.

Some day, please fate, I'll serve again
where she and the mountain wait,
In the land of *sayonara*
by that lonely Torii gate.

A PLACE THERE WAS
THAT KNEW MARINES

A place there was that knew Marines
        and heard their cadenced tread,
A ground that holds their footprints yet
        and shrouds their hallowed dead.

- - -

A place there was where pirates held
        Marines within a wall,
Until we marched the Sahara across
        to bring a tyrant's fall.

    A wall there was in Tripoli
    That circled Derne 'round,
    Until we hurled our charge at it
    And brought it crashing down.

A place there was in old Cathay
                    beneath the Tartar Wall,
That secrets old as China knew,
                    and kept them, kept them all.

        A way there was in Peking town,
        A street named *Hatamen*,
        That knew the fabled Horse Marines
        When they were lean, young men.

A place there was where bandits ruled
                    a broad-leafed, tropic world,
Until the day we landed there,
                    our battle flags unfurled.

        A vale there is in Haiti's hills
        Where, if you listen well,
        You still may hear the echo of
        A dying bandit's yell.

A place there was where German troops
    held half the world at bay,
Until the Leathernecks got there
    and slammed into the fray.

  A wood there was in shattered France
  Where, in the swirling fogs,
  The Germans met those dauntless men
  They nicknamed "Devil Dogs".

A place there was where *banzai* shouts
    tore tropic peace to shreds,
And ships and planes came constantly
    to throw death at our heads.

  A hill there was in "Great Lew Chew"
  Some west of Shuri's tower,
  Where Leathernecks won real estate
  At half a yard an hour.

A place there was where Chinese hordes
                    made life a fearsome chore,
While tired Marines fought valiantly
                    to reach a friendly shore.

        A road there was in old Korea,
        From Chosin to the sea,
        Where frozen in the ageless ice,
        Is deathless gallantry.

A place there was that knew Marines
                    in some far, distant scene.
A wood, a hill, a road, a wall,
                    a place -- that's where we've been.

Note: "Lew Chew" on page 23 was
probably a phonetic attempt at *Liu Chiu*, an
ancient name for Ryukyu, the island chain
that includes Okinawa.

THE BALLAD OF BENNY SAUL

If you were down at Guadalcanal
                  that hungry, bloody, fall,
Mayhap you knew a fightin' man
                  named Corporal Benny Saul.

Well, he wasn't quite a small man,
                  'though you wouldn't call him tall;
But a hell-for-leather Leatherneck
                  was Corporal Benny Saul.

We used up most all our rations
                  'cept sardines, oiled and tinned,
And mostly we griped and grumbled
                  But Benny Saul just grinned.

Between the fights we talked of home
               and cussed the stinkin' war,
But Benny Saul just smiled at us
               and talked about the Corps.

For Benny was a scrapper, of the
               breed that wins or dies;
And you could see the sheer, raw
               courage flashing in his deep-set eyes.

Our platoon set up an ambush
               out beyond the Tenaru,
And countin' the lieutenant
               we were down to twenty-two.

Even when a rifle squad
               T/O was just nine men,
A platoon with only twenty-two
               was spread out mighty thin.

We set in along a jungle trail
                    late that afternoon and
Hoped that, if we got a fight,
                    we'd get it started soon.

The Nip point sprung our trap
                    in the tender side of night
And we held fire until we had
                    their main force in our sight.

It lasted just a short while till
                    we started breaking free,
But if hell is any hotter
                    it's a Christian's life for me.

When we started breakin' contact
                    the night was coal-mine black
And we slammed head-on into
                    more Nips at our back!

Our lieutenant, cool as winter,
                        closed our circle tight;
But not one man among us thought
                    he'd live to see dawn's light.

Then Benny Saul he volunteered
                        to get back to our line,
And even in the black of night
                    that wolf-grin seemed to shine.

'Fore anyone could stop him
                    Corporal Saul was out of sight.
Then a single burst of *Nambu* fire
                        rip-sawed through the night.

It was near an hour later when
                        the *Banzai* charge began,
And now there was no doubtin'
                    we'd be slaughtered to the man!

When through the roaring firefight
        rang the street-fight battle cry.
"Hey, Marine!" echoed the shout
        over the Nips' *"Banzai!"*

Out in front of the counter attack,
        all cold steel and pure gall,
Came a ragin', slashin', fightin' man
        named Corporal Benny Saul.

Salutin' our lieutenant then,
        "I made it, Sir," he said;
And doing an about-face,
        pitched to the ground stone dead.

We rolled him over gently,
        lest we disturb his rest,
And counted seven bullet holes
        stitched across his chest!

No, we'd not thought him a big man,

            our Corporal Benny Saul;

But laid out in the jungle dawn

            he looked full ten feet tall.

THE PLACE OF ANGELS

The VC trained their biggest guns on us,
And rained a storm of steel on Con Thien.
The "Place of Angels" was a 'beaten zone',
Like several other places we have been.

It really had been pretty in the springtime,
All decked out in early green and gold;
And we had so much peace and quiet then
That even butterflies grew fat and bold.

But Charlie's guns plowed it up in autumn,
And the wet monsoon came on top of that.
Your 'hooch' became a covered wadin' pool
And your roommate was most usually a rat.

We took the 'incoming' and fat trench rats
And we survived the Ham-and-Lima Beans,
But sittin' dug in on a tiny hill
Is one hard job for attack-trained Marines.

A fighter's temper always tends to curdle
When all he can do is dig and hide,
And when the only foe is shells explodin',
It's a lot like shovin' sand against the tide.

Although we kept ol' Charlie off our hilltop,
And we can do it any time again,
If you don't mind, we'll fight out in the open,
And let the Angels back to Con Thien.

OLD MARINE

What Old Corps stories could you tell,
                    Old Marine, Old Marine,
Of other times and far-off wars
                    You have seen, you have seen?

A China doll who, long ago,

           Used to wait, used to wait,

"Liberty" for starboard watch, by

           Peking Gate, Peking Gate.

Chinese "Boxers" half insane, with

           Hate and fear, hate and fear;

And Welsh comrades who bore the title,

           Fusilier, Fusilier.

Banana trees in tropic climes,

           Lush and green, lush and green,

Where bandit gangs killed and died,

           Seldom seen, seldom seen.

Success in battle savored full,

        Tasting good, tasting good,

When you stopped the Kaiser's drive at

        Belleau Wood, Belleau Wood. *

A ridge in France, high-sloped and steep,

    Named Blanc Mont, named Blanc Mont,

Where once again Death grinned at you, a

        Fearsome haunt, fearsome haunt.

A five-inch turret's slamming jolt,

        Remembered well, remembered well,

With brass shell casings piling high,

        Hot as hell, hot as hell.

Lap-sided whaleboats ramming hard
                    On the beach, on the beach.
Head-high gun'les high to climb,
                    Hard to reach, hard to reach.

Old canvas leggings always laced
                    High and tight, high and tight.
Campaign hats at salty slant
                    'Gainst the light, 'gainst the light.

Desp'rate days, hard fought and fierce, when
                    No one knew, no one knew
If guts alone, on Midway Island, could
                    Pull you through, pull you through.

Fabled battles, always tough,

                    Often lean, often lean;

But soldiering a noble life,

                    Never mean, never mean.

Comrades lost so long ago

                    Marching by, marching by,

Sun-tanned faces young again to

                    Memory's eye, memory's eye.

"Faithful service," four decades, in

                    Peace and war, peace and war,

Spanned the globe twice around on

                    Ship and shore, ship and shore.

What distant climes and far-off wars
        Have you seen, have you seen?
What Old Corps stories could you tell,
        Old Marine, Old Marine?

*Belleau Wood was the first decisive Allied victory in World War One. The French re named it "Wood of the Marine Brigade" in tribute to the U.S. Fourth Marine Brigade.

ICEBERG IN THE SUBTROPICS

We stood out at dusk from Leyte
On a heading laid for Guam;
And though there was no typhoon,
You'd scarcely call it calm.

The crew looked somewhat greenish
And the troops were far from well;
The men who knew seasickness
Had found their private hell.

Before we'd sailed for half a week
We reached our rendevous,
With ships of every type and size,
A thousand -- maybe two.

Far out, somewhere beyond hull-down,
Coursed lethal ships of the line,
Cool, gray deadliness above
Warship hulls, sleek and fine.

There carriers and battleships
Prowled, numerous as stars --
An armada larger than ever seen
In all of Europe's wars.

And snuggled at the center
The wallowing troopships rode,
Almost unarmed and helpless,
Carrying the vital load.

Here rode the men whose deadly
Job it was to bring the war,
For the first time in those years,
To Nippon's own home shore.

Our goal was Okinawa
First of the Ryukyu Isles,
Which once was Nansei Shoto
And would be "Isle of Smiles."

There our first *Kamikaze*,
High in a deep azure sky,
Tipped a wing into a dive;
We watched him dive--and die.

Easter and April Fool's Day,
And then code-named "Love Day", too!
The ride in the landing craft
Was too peaceful to be true.

We went in on Bolo Point
And I didn't fire a round.
It seemed the island's safest spot
Was this beach we had found.

It went like that for near two weeks
As we swept toward the north.
A small firefight now and then
Was scarcely our money's worth.

But then when we hit Motobu
Things started to get right hot;
For two weeks more, all trench warfare,
Tough fighting would be our lot.

At last the peninsula fell
And we thought we'd get a rest,
But rest time is rare in combat;
Instead, we got a real test.

The Army at Shuri Line,
On the drive to Naha town,
Found the Japanese main force
And urged us to come on down.

Sent to the right of the line,
On the Machinato flank,
We found the Nips holdin' tough
On top of a steep-sloped bank.

It was smoke, steel, and sluggin'
Those next few long days--and hard.
Once we fought on Sugar Loaf
Twenty hours, for just *one* yard!

When Shuri-Machinato Line
Finally gave and went down,
We swept down Sugar Loaf Hill
And out into Naha town.

With scarce a brick on a brick,
Her destruction was complete.
The gentle, old city lay dead
In a rubble winding-sheet.

University buildings
Near the port, at Tomari;
And, south, a lone Torii gate
Were about all you could see.

We pushed on south to the cliffs
But that didn't happen soon!
The wet monsoon washed us down
Through most of May and June.

Tanks and 'dozers bogged in ooze
And walkin' was sticky-slow.
Our ear lobes greened with mildew;
Our toenails rusted below.

The fight grew ever tougher
As we slogged and bled and fell.
Guiltless natives, caught between,
Fled in terror, pell-mell.

Most of three long months we fought
To pack Okinawa in,
And we and the Japanese
Both lost a lot of good men.

But the natives, gentle souls,
Suffered the far graver dread.
Their towns were blown to the ground;
A hundred thousand lay dead!

"Iceberg"--the bloodiest fight
In that island-hopping war;
But the damn' thing was worth it,
It opened Japan's front door.

But a nightmare fight was next;
So we re-stocked and got set.
Then bombs on two Japanese towns
Stamped "cancel" on plans for that.

Spared the climb up "Olympus", *
We truly didn't much care.
"Iceberg" had cooled us down a bit;
So we were glad to stop there.

* The planned assault on Japan
was named *OLYMPIC*. American
casualties were projected to be *one
million!*

NIGHT AND LUKE THE GOOK

We were livin' in the trenches
                in the spring of '52,
And fightin' in the paddies
                and along the ridgelines, too.

Daylight seldom brought us much
                that you could call a fight--
Some mortars and artillery, but
                we did our work at night.

The bushes crawled and stalked you
                while your eyes strained fever-hot,
And some of them was bushes
                but some of them was not.

For snoopin' to your trenchline,
Old Luke, he liked the dark;
So we polished up our night skills
and joined him for a lark.

If you fancy you're a *bon vivant*
when strolling in the park,
Just wait 'til you've met Luke
out in the paddies after dark.

He's quiet and most hard to find
and fearsome hard to pin,
But wherever you smell garlic
is a place where he has been.

So we sat out by the paddy dikes
and scouted by the wood,
And whenever we could find Luke
we mostly whipped him good.

But don't go thinkin' he's easy
                    or that he couldn't fight.
Luke taught some deadly lessons
                    'til we learned to fight at night.

But even when we thought we'd learned
                    and made some handsome gains,
Sometimes Luke would outsit us
                    and whomp us for our pains.

"ALL QUIET ON THE UN FRONT"
                    "Patrol Action Is Light"
Headlines written by a man
                    who never fought at night.

For a little fight's a big one
                    when it happens where you are,
And if it comes at nighttime,
                    "light action" is a war!

Yes, we lived out in the trenches,

        and mostly fought at night;

And one thing that we surely learned--

        no nighttime fight is light.

Exciting it most always is,

        or furious, or hot,

And sometimes purely thrilling;

        but *light* it just is not!

So if you'd romp with Lukey,

        (and who knows when you might?)

Learn to work in darkness; then

        stand by to fight at night.

A SUFFERING CALLED VALLEY FORGE

We wintered there in crackling cold
                    at a place called Valley Forge,
Marines ashore as cannoneers in
                    the army of General George.

No place for soldiers of the sea,

        that frigid, snowy, dell.

The wind, unlike the balmy trades,

        was cold as billy-blue-hell!

In we went from holy-stoned decks

        to mud, and slush, and snow,

While the citizen soldiers slipped away

        and *esprit* was lower than low.

Yet, in spite of dwindling spirits

        and hardships handed out free,

There stayed in that hell of frostbite

        and pain, those heroes yet to be.

None cried out from the bloodied stains
                    of their footprints in the snow,
But a cheer they raised for Washington
                    in every place he'd go.

Somehow the frost-hard winter passed
                    and spring burst flower bright,
And the swelling of the leaflets
                    brought the fledgling army's might.

From there to Guilford Courthouse,
                    all up and down the land,
The war raged four more bloody years
                    before it reached its end.

Muskets laid smoke in the valleys
                    and rattled across the hills,
While orators made speeches that
                    would give a senator chills.

I learned of heroes in those years
                    of following General George,
But none more brave or true I saw
                    than those at Valley Forge.

For they were no sunshine soldiers
                    but men with a patriot's dream,
Whose courage full matched their vision
                    and who chose to *be*, not to *seem*.

THINK TWICE OF THE INFANTRY

Think twice, think twice of the Infantry,
Think twice a'fore you sign,

For the "foot Marines" is a hard way of life
Where there's boots and brass to shine;
And a rifle a man must treat like a wife,
And tents you must pitch in a line.

And you'll fry in tin hats 'neath a tropic sun
Hot as the "hinges" below;
And you'll empty a ton of sand from your boots
And roll out to sleep in the snow.

Think twice, think twice of the Infantry,
Think twice of the forester green,

For the way seems long and ofttimes rough
And the sergeants gruff and mean;
And the hikes stretch long and dusty-tough
For the young, first-cruise Marine.

And the men you'll learn to love like kin
Are a doughty, stiff-necked crew,
Who look with scorn on all other men
But would risk their lives for you.

Think twice, think twice of the Infantry,
Think twice of "Battle's Queen",

For the Infantry must walk to its fight
And a firefight's no game on the green;
And there are no innings, day or night,
For the bone-tired "mud" Marine.

No matter how tired or hungry you be
You must learn to take it in stride,
For there's no walking out on the Infantry;
She's jealous as any new bride.

Think twice, think twice of the Infantry,
Think twice of the sons of the sword,

For these are hard men who come from the sea
With a grim and deadly accord;
And there are no babes in the Infantry--
The name's a poor-chosen word.

Yes, lad, think twice of the Infantry,
Think twice of St. Michael's clan,
For if you serve in the Infantry
You'll serve with men, as a man.

CHARLEMAGNE PERALTE
AND SGT. HANNEKEN

When we first went into Haiti
                    it didn't look too bad.
A gang of untrained bandits was
                    all the foe we had.

But, though they were ill-organized,
                    with little chance to train,
They held a damn' good hole card in
                    their leader, Charlemagne.

He was wily, bold, and daring, and
                    was raisin' plenty hob;
So our President sent the Marines
                    to "pacify" that mob.

We went ashore right cheerfully
                    to this banana shoot,
For pacifying bandits was
                    our second strongest suit.

Our forces had been beefed up
                    with local *gendarmerie*,
Whose knowledge of the jungle was
                    a pretty thing to see.

We beat the brush for Charlemagne
                    without too much success,
'Cause where the bandit chief might be
                    was anybody's guess.

Firefights we had aplenty
                and a bad ambush or two,
But each time we'd find Charlemagne
                he'd vanish like the dew.

At last we found his hide-out
                in a hilly, wooded glen,
But to take that bandit stronghold
                we'd have lost a hundred men.

'Twas then that Sergeant Hanneken
                came up with his plan;
He'd go into the hideout dressed
                as Charlemagne's own man!

There were sev'ral others of us
                who went up with Hanneken,
'Though thinkin' back, we only had
                a bare handful of men.

One man and Hanneken went in
                dressed like that bandit crew;
And it was hairy, scary business,
                I don't mind telling you.

The rest stopped in the shadows
                where the firelight glow began,
While Hanneken walked forward
                to the center of the clan.

And stopping only when he stood
                before that wild chieftain,
He whipped his pistol up and fired--
                point-blank at Charlemagne!

Peralte's arms flew outward and
                he death-leaped toward the sky,
While we set up a racket like
                the Fourth day of July!

We sounded like an army shootin'
in that ghostly glen,
And panic shook the wits out of
Charlemagne's scared men.

They raced out from that clearing
as from the gates of hell,
And it grew plumb deathly quiet
in that spooky, ink-black dell.

Of the force that had been reckoned
at least 1200 men,
There remained now in the stronghold
just their dead chief, Charlemagne.

But that's not the whole story of
the steely-nerved Marine
Who walked into that bandit camp
and killed old Charlemagne.

A much-respected hero,
Hanneken would travel far.
By the time he hung his sword up
he wore a general's star.

PAK, DUK SOO

He wasn't much to look at,
                like Kipling's "Gunga Din",
'Though his uniform was
                more complete by far.

He'd scrounged Marine utilities
                from several of the men,
This man the young Marines
                called "Captain Scar."

A solid chunk of granite, with
                a reckless, hard-faced stare,
He stood not one inch
                over five-foot-two,

Yet he marched 'longside our troops
                with a salty, cheerful air,
Our old Korean "talker",
                Pak, Duk Soo.

A jagged mark across his cheek
                        looked like a sabre slash
And accounted for the
                        nickname, "Captain Scar".

He never told a soul I knew
                        just how he'd got that gash,
But I liked to think 'twas
                        some old bandit war.

If the colonel didn't need him
                        when we were on the move,
You'd see him range the column,
                        near and far.

Movin' with the troops
                        seemed to be his only love,
Our brown-faced, grinnin',
                        talker, Captain Scar.

We relieved some KMC*
        on a hill that looked sky-high,
With "Luke's Castle"
        not a pistol shot away.

The Chinese sounded *reveille*
        while night still stained the sky
And a screamin' charge
        began our every day.

One wintry morn the colonel
        came up front to watch the show;
And, of course, right by his side
        was Pak, Duk Soo.

That day 'twas not the token charge
        that we had come to know.
Despite our heavy fire,
        the gooks broke through.

* Korean Marine Corps

They swept into our trenches
        like a floodtide o'er the beach
And isolated those
        in our OP.

It was touch and go there for awhile,
        the OP out of reach,
Before we could turn back
        that dust-brown sea.

Just as we came bustin' through
        to pull the colonel out
Four Chinese made a try
        to reach him, too.

The colonel's pistol failed to fire
        and I heard someone shout.
Then straight into those four
        charged Pak, Duk Soo!

He was a screamin', ragin', terror,
                          racin' through the snow,
With a bayonet he'd got
                          from Lord knows who.

In his charge he speared three enemy
                          who simply moved too slow,
And I shot one,
                          but that one shot Duk Soo.

He grinned that reckless, hard-faced grin
                          when I knelt down to see,
But his eyes were seein' something
                                    sad and deep.

I bent down close to hear him say,
                "They killed my son, Duk Lee,"
And with those words
                          he seemed to go to sleep.

71

Now sometimes on a long march,
                    the column strung out far,
I think that I can see him
                    marchin', too.

He's grinnin' like he always did
                    and fingerin' that scar,
Our old Third Battalion talker,
                    Pak, Duk Soo.

I don't know who his god was,
                    or if he ever prayed.
It seems likely that
                    he worshipped *Dai Butsu.**

But, if he should be listening,
                    that god who Pak's fate made,
I'd ask him for good duty
                    for our old friend, Pak, Duk Soo.

*Buddha in Japanese, spoken by most Koreans
in the 1950's, after 50 years of Japanese rule

AND SPEAK NOT OF GLORY

Oh, how can they speak of glory
Who have not fought and bled,
Who have seen snow black with cinders
But never splashed bloody red?

It's easy to say, "Ah, brave young men!"
And feel the pulse thrill and race,
If you've never left the fires of home
To look into Death's hoary face.

There was glory a'plenty at Chosin
Though no one spoke the word there,
Where the shatterin' cold of Korea
Made frost in your beard's coarse hair.

The Chinese offered dishonor
In exchange for warmth and bread.
The rear files shouted, "To hell with you!"
And shouting, fought and bled.

The North Wind shrieked with laughter
And cut through and back again.
The front files cried out, "We're freezing!"
And freezing, fought to win.

The ridgelines were black with enemy
Numerous as Khan's yellow tide.
They rose and charged the Leathernecks--
Charged, met steel--and died.

Again the horde spilled down those hills;
Again, and a hundred times more.
And the Leathernecks, lamed with frostbite,
Hacked through them to the shore.

So, speak not lightly of glory
Who have not fought and bled,
For glory sits not at the hearthside
Nor snuggles all warm in your bed.

She waits to be wooed in some far-off land,
In jungles and paddies and sich;
And it's cold steel and guts that'll win 'er,
For Glory's a bloodthirsty bitch!

DON'T GO WALKIN' IN A'SHAU VALLEY

If you go walkin' in A'shau Valley,
           take a brigade or two.
It can get damn' lonely in A'shau
        when there's only Charlie and you.

Old Charlie thinks he owns the place
          and he's right jealous of it;
So should he find you in 'his' valley
        he's likely to kill you a bit.

Well, we walked out in A'shau Valley
         a half-dozen times or more,
And every time Charlie acted like
        we hadn't stomped him before.

We brought out gear he'd stashed in caves,
        guns and ammo and such;
Goods of war aimed at Hue and Da Nang--
        you'd never believe how much.

Of course, it wasn't a shoppin' spree
        'cause Charlie was also in there,
Hosin' us down with AK-47's
        and RPG's ever'where.

But we took plenty of muscle in,
        plus air and artillery;
And each time again we whomped Charlie
        when we walked in A'Shau Valley.

But, don't *you* go walkin' in A'Shau
        unless life holds no appeal.
That valley means so much to Charlie
        he'll shoot your hide full of steel.

THOSE MAGNIFICENT MEN
(and their flying machines)

When Cunningham, in 1911,
　　　　　first taxied "Noisy Nan",
He may have been the lone Marine
　　　　　who knew what just began.

The doughty young lieutenant
　　　　　and his noisy plane went far;
In five short years Marines flew in
　　　　　"The War To End All War".

And Cunningham early foresaw
                    the later, greater dream
That spawned the now battle-honed
                    Marine Corps air-ground team.

Throughout the Caribbean Sea
                    in the 'Banana Wars',
Men like Schilt and Geiger made
                    the airplane part of our Corps.

Flying open-cockpit planes
                    they founded air support,
Ferrying beans and bandages
                    or strafing some bandit fort.

DUNNAGAN

By World War II, close air support
                was a Marine Corps art,
Polished in small jungle wars
                by men of vision and heart.

At Midway and Guadalcanal
                they faced enormous odds,
Where they fought Homeric air battles
                in planes kissed by the gods.

For only the *men* were ready when
                the dogs of war were loosed.
Machines they flew to the 40's war
                were planes the 30's had used.

Then came a plane designed to fill
                a fighter pilot's dream,
The dazzling, gull-winged Corsair,
                wild as a banshee scream.

Though the autogiro failed
                    in its Banana Wars test,
Marines turned to its next-of-kin,
                    an unseemly aircraft at best.

When Korea brought *police action*
                    Marines were ready again.
They had nurtured the helicopter
                    and another new era began.

The aging Corsair carried on
                    as wheelhorse at the start,
And copters set us on hilltops
                    high enough to burst your heart.

The graceful gull wing then gave way
        to the fierce jet engine's roar,
While choppers moved troops and casualties
        at speeds undreamed of before.

At last the non-war ground to a halt
        without reaching an end,
And Marines who took to the air in
        machines, sought new skies to win.

DUNNAGANG

Early in 1962, one of them
         owned the world for a day,
And a line formed behind John Glenn
         on the march to the Milky Way.

Now and next year and through decades
         still out among the stars,
They'll swear by, and at, the machines
         they fly, training for future wars.

For it isn't the jets or bug-smashers
         that make a flying Marine,
Who's a breed of man that sings raucous
         songs and is part of his machine.

From Cunningham, Schilt, and Geiger,

        Boyington, Foss, and Glenn,

To teenage boys who dream of the sky,

        they're a "right stuff" kind of men.

The thing that makes them different,

        these fliers who wear Marine green,

Is that first, before flying, or walking,

        or what, a Marine is--a Marine.

DUNNAGAN

CITADEL ON THE PERFUME RIVER

The people of Hue held aloof from the war,
            As becomes a cultural breed.
They studied, and painted, and sculpted,
        And wrote, but eschewed political creed.

Their attitude toward both sides it seemed,
          Was, "Ignore them; they'll go away."
Then the VC came and raped the town
            On their holy New Year's Day!

Hue citizens couldn't believe such a thing--
    That Charlie would rake them with fire,
Bringing the war to their Citadel,
        Making Hue a funeral pyre.

For the Citadel was sacrosanct,
        As was the whole city of Hue;
And perhaps the most sacred day of the year
        Was *Tet*, their New Year's Day.

Marine Task Force X-ray moved up from
        Da Nang to counter-attack into Hue,
And we swept the Perfume River's south bank
        In not much more than a day.

Then we started across the long river bridge
    To retake the old Citadel,
When Charlie's machineguns opened fire
    And the steel bridge rang like a bell!

It was get-the-hell-off that naked steel
    And scoot back to solid ground,
For we couldn't shoot our way across
    Without destroying the old town.

So, we sat 'twixt a rock and a hard place,
    With clouds hangin' low as a man;
And that night while we waited for dawn,
    Charlie's sappers blew the main span!

No bridge, no choppers, artillery or air,
        And us on the river's wrong side!
We felt like the girl who complained,
        "A bridesmaid, but never a bride."

Well, the Perfume River don't smell like
        perfume, at least none I've ever seen.
It was full of debris, dead bodies and trash,
        And was scummy and slimy-green.

But we hadn't come for the scenery
        And in time we made it across.
By pontoon 'n small boat 'n copter 'n such,
        We went to show Charlie his boss.

The weather throughout was too bad for air,
          And they ruled out artillery;
So, re-taking the town, as it usually does,
          Fell squarely to infantry.

The battle was ours when the last shot was
   Fired and, although some damage was done,
The city of Hue and the old Citadel
          Lay peaceful again 'neath the sun.

Back home some blamed *us* for fightin' there.
          We ravaged the city, they say;
But 'they' are liars, ignoring the facts--
   Vietnamese raped and murdered poor Hue!

Marines held the big guns out of the town
        To avoid undue damage there.
Our blood and torn flesh won the Citadel;
  So it still stands, that damn' dusty square.

The Perfume flows serene through Hue City,
      With debris, trash, and bodies removed.
The Citadel hides its war scars in shame,
    While we mourn the comrades we loved.

VERSE ON A WARRIOR'S HELMET

As the roots of the seedling oak tree
      grow strong in the toss of a storm,
So mankind in war gathers strength
      for growth that in peacetime had no form.

Progress conceived in easier times
        while lulled the adrenal gland,
Is spawned a lusty manchild when
        the sword's shadow lies on the land.

Ideas birthed in time of peace
        oft perish of relaxation's 'germ'.
Only in springtime's upheaval does
        the butterfly come from the 'worm'.

War, though mankind's greatest dread
        and civilization's affront,
Fits nature's first rule for balance--
        that the hunted must also hunt.

For wartime's urgent drive to win
          sends mankind bounding ahead,
And the greatest advances man has made
          have been of chaos bred.

Man is true child of nature;
          he must have a challenge to meet.
Cursing war, he gives it his all,
          yet in peace may lift not his feet.

So war, as all of life's curses, often
          blesses those it has cursed.
In reducing life to the basics
          war brings the best from the worst.

That best is man's compassion,

        his boundless capacity for love;

And it's only in Mars' grim shadow

        that man truly woos the dove.

So the curse may be also a blessing,

        despite the killing and hate;

For humans warm by the hearthside,

        let progress and brotherhood wait.

BENEDICTION

Here's health to you and to our Corps, which
we are proud to serve;
In many a strife we've fought for life
and never lost our nerve.

(From verse three, The Marines' Hymn. Anon.)